NOR: PP

Face of ___

a play in one act by Jack Booth

Characters

(In order of appearance)

Trisha Stanton

Kay Lawrence

Clive, her husband

Philip, Trisha's husband

DCI Dunne

DS Rose

The action takes place in the Stantons' house on the outskirts of Dalebury, a northern market town.

Time: *The early 1990's. An early evening in late autumn.*

1

Face of Evil

The scene is the Stantons' lounge. A door R opens off the entrance-hall. There is a window UC in the rear wall with the curtains drawn closed. The essential items of furniture are an easy-chair RC, a settee LC (both facing an imaginary fireplace in the "fourth wall") and a drinks table against the L wall - any further items are optional and for set-dressing purposes. There could be a lit floor and/or table lamp and a vase(s) of autumn flowers.

As the curtain rises there is a BURST OF LAUGHTER onstage.

TRISHA STANTON is sitting in the easy-chair with KAY and CLIVE LAWRENCE side by side on the settee. The LAWRENCEs are in their mid/late 30's with TRISHA a few years younger. The two women are wearing evening dresses and the man a formal suit. All three are holding partly-empty cocktail glasses and the general atmosphere is relaxed.

TRISHA: *(laughing)* That was very good, Clive.

CLIVE: *(smiling confidently)* Yes, I thought so.

KAY: *(not prudishly)* If rather near the knuckle. Usually you're far more restrained.

CLIVE: *(with a degree of familiarity)* It's Trish... brings out the beast in me. *(drinks.)*

KAY: *(to Trisha)* Do tell! Nowadays I rarely bring out his best... and that isn't much of a recommendation, believe me.

TRISHA: Kay! I'm quite sure that Clive has hidden depths.

KAY: If he has I've never plumbed them. Perhaps we should change places... I've always quite fancied Philip.

TRISHA: *(smiling)* For heaven's sake don't let him hear that. It'll make him even more unbearable!

(ALL laugh quietly and sip their drinks as the door R opens and PHILIP STANTON ENTERS. PHILIP is in his late 30's, also formally dressed. He looks serious.)

KAY: *(brightly)* Philip, you've missed a funny story from Clive - and really quite naughty.

PHILIP: *(soberly)* I hope it was better than those he used to tell in the Officers'

Mess.

TRISHA: *(half-turning)* Darling, is something the matter?

PHILIP: It's the Police. *(Turning to speak to off R through the open doorway)* Please come in.

(DCI DUNNE ENTERS R followed by DS ROSE. DUNNE is a middle-aged man with an unorthodox manner and a somewhat droll sense of humour. He is well, if not impeccably, dressed, possibly with an unfastened car coat and perhaps a scarf. DS ROSE is female, in her early 30's, casually but stylishly dressed, possibly in slacks and leather jacket. She is carrying a large envelope.)

(indicating Trisha) This is my wife... *(indicating Kay and Clive)* Mr and Mrs Lawrence, they're friends of ours. We were in the Army together.

KAY: *(with a smile)* I was only an Army wife. *(giving Dunne a questioning look as he stares at her.)*

DUNNE: I'm sorry. Was I staring?

KAY: Yes, you were.

DUNNE: *(embarrassed)* It's just that I...

KAY: *(not offended)* Please don't apologise... er?

PHILIP: This is Inspector...?

DUNNE: Dunne, sir, as I said when you opened the door... Detective Chief Inspector Dunne. This is Detective Sergeant Rose - a rose amongst the rest of us C.I.D. thorns. Isn't that so, Sergeant?

ROSE: *(quietly polite)* As you say, sir.

DUNNE: *(to the others)* The Sergeant has heard my little joke before.

ROSE: Many times, sir.

PHILIP: *(to Dunne)* You must excuse me, Inspector... faces I rarely forget but I really am quite hopeless at remembering names - as my wife will confirm.

TRISHA: Quite hopeless... *(with a wry smile)* and not only with names!

PHILIP: I didn't introduce myself, did I? I'm Philip....

DUNNE: Stanton.

PHILIP: *(surprised)* That's right. I don't believe we've met before.

DUNNE: And you never forget a face? No, sir, our paths have never crossed. Hardly surprising as I'm sure we've never been going in the same direction.

KAY: Are you psychic, Inspector?

DUNNE: I very much doubt it... though it might come in useful at times, eh, Sergeant?

ROSE: Very useful, sir.

DUNNE: *(to Philip)* No, it's all those posters plastered around the town.

CLIVE: *(sardonically)* Wanted... Dead or Alive!

KAY: The photograph doesn't really do him justice. What do you say, Trisha?

PHILIP: *(to Dunne)* You mean the Bye-Election poster? I was forgetting.

DUNNE: "Vote for Stanton".

KAY: Shall you, Inspector?

PHILIP: Steady on, Kay! This is not a canvassing session.

DUNNE: I'm afraid I'm one of those awkward sods - pardon the expression, ladies... not my Sergeant, she already knows. *(ROSE smiles.)* I'm referring to the politicians' nightmare - the floating voter who can't make up his - or her - mind. I never can - not until the last minute - not about most things. The wife calls it my congenital defect... amongst others!

TRISHA: So you're married?

DUNNE: Very much so, ma'am. *(to Philip)* No, sir, I have to admit I never know where to put my cross on the voting paper. It's as if I'm waiting for either divine inspiration or a last-minute revelation of some juicy bit of scandal concerning one of the candidates. That would do the trick... polarize my thoughts...

CLIVE: Rule him out of contention?

DUNNE: No chance, sir, he'd be certain of my vote.

KAY: *(laughing)* There you are, Philip. Now you know what to do.

PHILIP: I shall need a hell of a lot more votes than that! *(with a change of tone)* But I'm quite sure you didn't come here to discuss politics, Inspector?

DUNNE: No, sir, not my favourite topic of conversation, if you'll pardon me.

PHILIP: *(pointedly looking at his wristwatch)* The thing is we are a bit pressed

4

for time.

DUNNE: *(profusely apologetic)* Are you, sir? Oh, I am sorry, you should have said. Here I've been rabbiting on...

PHILIP: We were having a drink before going out for a meal. *(moving to drinks table L)* I don't suppose...? No, of course not - you'll be on duty, won't you? *(picks up his partly-empty glass)*

DUNNE: I'm afraid so.

PHILIP: A bit late in the day, isn't it?

DUNNE: Time waits for no man... *(with a nod towards Rose)* or woman. *(as PHILIP raises his glass to drink)* Not where murder is concerned!

(PHILIP checks and puts glass down. TRISHA reacts nervously.)

KAY: *(purely out of interest)* Murder!? Who's been murdered?

DUNNE: If I could tell you that, madame, it's unlikely that we should be here.

CLIVE: Aren't you being unnecessarily mysterious?

DUNNE: *(firmly)* I'm not responsible for the mystery... only unfortunately with the task of clearing it up - if at all possible.

PHILIP: *(interjecting)* Look, Inspector, if it will help us to get to the point - I think I know the reason you're here. *(becoming the focus of attention)*

DUNNE: Do you, sir?

PHILIP: Isn't it in connection with the body that was found locally... a month or so ago, wasn't it?

DUNNE: It is indeed.

KAY: What body is that? You haven't mentioned it, Philip.

PHILIP: *(vaguely)* Haven't I? I don't suppose I thought you'd be interested. You or Clive.

DUNNE: It was a male body, ma'am. You haven't read about it?

CLIVE: My wife and I don't live around here. We're from Sussex.

DUNNE: *(drily)* By the sea!

CLIVE: Just inland actually - near Chichester.

DUNNE: And very nice too. Then you're only visiting?

KAY: Giving Philip moral support... the Bye-Election.

PHILIP: Much needed!

KAY: You were saying, Inspector?

DUNNE: Was I?

KAY: About the body.

DUNNE: Oh yes. It was discovered out at Bagshaw's Farm up on the Crabtree Road. Perhaps you know it?

CLIVE: It's our first visit to Dalebury. We've been intending to come up for quite some time - to see my old Army mate.

PHILIP: Less of the "old"!

CLIVE: But my wife's filming commitments have ruled otherwise. She's so rarely at home... the perfect set-up for an ideal marriage.

DUNNE: Filming? Of course!

ROSE: *(discreetly)* It's Kay Kingsley, sir.

DUNNE: Yes, of course it is. It was the name...

KAY: I was born Kay Scraggs, but....

DUNNE: Yes, I see.

KAY: The alliteration is supposed to work wonders... Bridget Bardot..., Marilyn Monroe..., Sharon Stone...

DUNNE: Minnie Mouse?

KAY: At least it did for them. I'm not so sure about Minnie! So it was found at this farm?

DUNNE: Yes, a chap was ploughing with a tractor and dug up an arm.

TRISHA: How awful!

DUNNE: Must have given him a nasty shock. The farmer notified the police and the rest of the body was found in a shallow grave... which is where Sergeant Rose and myself came into the picture - and a far from pretty one, *(to Rose)* was it?

ROSE: Not pretty at all, sir.

PHILIP: Earlier you mentioned murder.

DUNNE: No doubt about that, sir. The body was badly decomposed and the head damaged by the plough. Nevertheless the Home Office pathologist was able to clearly identify dents at the back of the skull - almost certainly inflicted by the familiar "blunt instrument".

CLIVE: Which has not been found?

DUNNE: *(with alertness)* Why do you say that, sir?

CLIVE: I assumed that if it had you might have said so.

DUNNE: I might... *(cryptically)* but then again I might not. *(more briskly)* However, you're quite right, sir. Whatever it was has not been found... as yet.

KAY: Who was he?

DUNNE: That, ma'am, is, as they say, the 64,000 dollar question. Who indeed?

CLIVE: Hasn't anyone reported him missing?

DUNNE: *(shaking his head)* It's as if he was an alien from another planet. The body was naked and without any distinguishing features - at least none that could still be ascertained. *(as an afterthought)* Oh, there was one thing - a gold stud in the right ear.

ROSE: *(quietly but firmly)* It was the left, sir.

DUNNE: Was it? *(to the others)* What would I do without her!?

PHILIP: It hardly sounds as if you've very much to go on.

DUNNE: That's an understatement if there was one... no name - no motive - no killer. Talk about drawing a blank - this is a double blank.

PHILIP: *(tersely)* You must excuse me, Chief Inspector, but I fail to see the reason for your visit. Am I to take it that I am in some way under suspicion?

TRISHA: Philip!

DUNNE: Is there any reason why you should be?

CLIVE: *(to Philip)* I shouldn't answer that, old man!

DUNNE: No, the Sergeant and I are grasping at straws... making house-to-house enquiries in the vain hope that someone somewhere may know something - some lead that might help us to identify who Alexander is... or was.

KAY: But you said...

DUNNE: It's the Superintendent's idea... full of them he is. He's called it

"Operation Alexander" - don't ask me why! It certainly has been quite an operation so far. In addition to the pathologist there's been an entomologist, a forensic archaeologist, an odontologist and a medical illustrator. The only person missing is Uncle Tom Cobley. *(ROSE grins.)*

PHILIP: I must say I'm surprised that you appear to be treating the matter so lightly. A man has been murdered, Inspector.

DUNNE: I'm well aware of that, sir. But believe you me if I wasn't able to indulge in the occasional smile, by this time it would be a question of tears - tears of frustration.

CLIVE: *(sympathetically)* Not making much headway, eh, Inspector?

DUNNE: It's been like trying to drive a car with the handbrake on. At least we now have a likely date of death - on or around September 25th.

PHILIP: As accurately as that?

DUNNE: The entomologist was supplied with maggots and larvae from the body.

(There is general reaction from all except ROSE.)

CLIVE: *(protesting)* Really, Inspector! There are two ladies present!

DUNNE: *(quietly)* Three, sir, actually. And Mr Stanton *did* ask.

CLIVE: *(blustering)* Yes, well... my apologies to your Sergeant. But I feel sure that we'd all be obliged for being spared the gory details.

KAY: *(to him)* I'd have thought you'd be only too interested as a writer of crime novels.

DUNNE: Really, sir? Under your own name?

CLIVE: I don't believe in my wife's alliteration theory. Have you read any of my stuff?

DUNNE: I'm afraid not, sir. But then I don't get much opportunity to read - other than official documents and reports. And this case has produced plenty of those. Don't understand how some of these professional types do it. For instance the odontologist chap, working from what teeth the plough left intact, was able to fix Alexander's age as being in his early forties - must be something like counting the rings on a tree-trunk.

TRISHA: I should think it would be far more scientific than that.

DUNNE: I'm sure you're right. Not only that, one molar on the left... am I right,

Sergeant?

ROSE: Right, sir. *(confirming)* It was on the left.

DUNNE: *(after glancing at her)* Had been crowned in metal - probably gold from an item of melted-down jewellery. This dental work suggested to the odontologist that it had been carried out either in East Europe or possibly Asia - with a liking for it being the former.

CLIVE: Shades of Sherlock Holmes!

DUNNE: Yes indeed, sir. Finally - although in practice this work was given priority - a medical illustrator reconstructed the face. I won't go into details, as fascinating as they are.

TRISHA: *(fervently)* Thank Heavens for that!

DUNNE: And then the newly-reconstructed face was photographed and computer-generated to give it black hair.

KAY: *(bluntly)* Why?

DUNNE: I forgot to mention that, when examining the shallow grave, the archaeologist recovered a single strand of black hair.

PHILIP: It's almost macabre beyond belief!

DUNNE: Indeed it is, sir... a forensic jigsaw puzzle the facts of which are stranger than fiction - without any reference to Mr Lawrence's writing being intended.

CLIVE: *(smiling)* No offence taken!

DUNNE: So now we know beyond any shadow of doubt - at least according to my information - exactly what poor Alexander looked like before he met his untimely end. *(to Philip)* Sergeant Rose will now show you and your wife a copy of that photograph. I shall be pleased if you will both study it carefully and say whether or not you have seen such a man recently around these parts - or for that matter elsewhere at any time in the past. *(with a nod to ROSE, who takes a 10" by 8" photograph out of the envelope and, approaching Philip, holds it out towards him.)*

PHILIP: *(after taking it and carefully looking before shaking his head)* No, I've never seen anyone like that. *(giving the photograph back to Rose)*

DUNNE: Are you quite sure, sir? You did say you never forget a face.

PHILIP: *(rather testily)* Yes, I'm sure. I said so, didn't I?

(ROSE moves to hold the photograph in front of TRISHA, who starts to reach out to take it then checks and gives an involuntary gasp.)

ROSE: *(quickly)* Do you know him, Mrs Stanton?

TRISHA: *(staring at the photograph as if hypnotized)* What? No, no, I don't know him. It's that face... a face of evil!

DUNNE: Yes, hardly one you'd want to come face-to-face with on a dark night. Or on second thoughts that might be the best time - far less visible!

KAY: May I see it?

CLIVE: *(brusquely)* For God's sake why, Kay? We weren't here.

KAY: I know that. Let's just say I'm curious. *(to Dunne)* May I? *(DUNNE nods to ROSE, who hands her the photograph. With a slight shudder)* Yes, Trisha, I can see what you mean. No, Inspector, I'd rather not meet him - even on a dark night.

DUNNE: Hardly likely to now, are you, ma'am?

KAY: *(showing him the photograph)* What do you think, Clive?

CLIVE: *(with barely a glance before rising)* I think that should conclude this visit. Mr Stanton and his wife both say they've never seen him.

DUNNE: What about you, sir?

CLIVE: What do you mean... what about me?

DUNNE: Have you ever seen him?

CLIVE: How the devil could I have? Apparently he was dead before we got here.

KAY: Calm down, darling. *(holding out the photograph for ROSE to take and put back into the envelope)*

DUNNE: *(calmly)* I meant while he was still alive. It is, after all, a small world - as my dear old Mum used to say. *(to Rose after there is no response)* Well, Sergeant, I think Mr Lawrence is right... we really shouldn't keep these people any longer from their evening meal. Don't know about you but I'm feeling peckish myself. "Never outstay your welcome," is what Mum used to tell me, "That's the secret of not taking undue advantage of hospitality... knowing when to leave".

PHILIP: It sounds as if your mother was a wise woman, Inspector.

DUNNE: That she was, sir. Pity I take after my father.

CLIVE: *(sarcastically)* She certainly seems to have been quite a conversationalist.

DUNNE: *(without taking offence)* Very voluble, sir. Dad used to say the only reason he went to work instead of staying at home and drawing the dole was to get a bit of peace and quiet.

TRISHA: *(naively)* What was he - a librarian?

DUNNE: *(amused)* He worked one of those pneumatic drills. Moaned that it tended to make him spill his beer *(quivering a hand)*. She used to tell him there was no good crying over spilt beer... always had to have the last word, Mum did.

PHILIP: *(pointedly looking at his watch)* Well, Inspector, I'm sorry we haven't been able to help you. *(moving towards the door R)* Let me show you and your Sergeant out.

DUNNE: Thank you, sir. *(starting to move R then checking)* Oh, there is just one thing, sir. Probably nothing to it... something you can explain easily. But the Superintendent is such a stickler, as my Sergeant will confirm. "Albert", he says - and I find it ominous when he calls me that - "Albert, attention to detail, leaving no stone unturned - that's the secret of successful police work".

PHILIP: *(impatiently)* Yes, I'm quite sure it is.

CLIVE: *(protesting)* Philip...!

PHILIP: *(to Dunne with a calming hand gesture to Clive)* Two minutes, Inspector.

DUNNE: Thank you. It's the elderly lady - further down the road on the other side... the one with the large black dog.

TRISHA: It's a Labrador.

PHILIP: Miss Braithwaite.

DUNNE: There, you see, sir? You remembered her name! Well, the thing is she told Sergeant Rose that she'd seen a man resembling the photograph. *(to Rose)* isn't that so, Sergeant?

ROSE: That was what she said, sir. Said she was quite sure.

CLIVE: But you said that nobody had seen him.

DUNNE: Did I? *(looking at Rose; to Clive)* What I think I said was that nobody knows who he was... *(turning to Philip)* that is, unless Mr Stanton can oblige?

PHILIP: What the devil do you mean? I said I'd never seen him, didn't I?

DUNNE: That was what you said, sir. But Miss Braithwaite thinks otherwise.

PHILIP: *(incredulously)* Thinks otherwise!? What does the old biddy know about it?

ROSE: She told me she'd seen you in conversation with him.

PHILIP: *(as TRISHA reacts)* What!? Where? When?

ROSE: Outside this house, sir. Late one evening.

PHILIP: Which evening?

ROSE: Miss Braithwaite wasn't sure... except that it was fairly recently.

PHILIP: *(scathingly)* No wonder she isn't sure. She must be off her trolley!

ROSE: That wasn't the impression she gave me. I'd say that for her age she's exceptionally clear-minded.

PHILIP: I've never heard such a load of rubbish! Exactly what did she tell you?

DUNNE: *(as ROSE looks at him)* She told Sergeant Rose that she was out walking her dog late one evening before retiring for the night. As she passed she saw you talking to him by the front door.

KAY: But wouldn't it have been dark?

ROSE: *(nodding her head)* She said it was and that you probably hadn't seen her in a dark-coloured coat with a black dog and without a street lamp at this point. But she said your outside security lamp was on... that she saw his face quite distinctly and that once seen...

CLIVE: *(interrupting)* From the street? What age is she?

ROSE: I'd say approaching eighty but apparently she still drives her car - and with a clean licence.

TRISHA: And the other man was my husband?

DUNNE: *(as ROSE hesitates)* She assumes that it was.

KAY: Assumes?

ROSE: According to her the other man was standing in shadow. All she saw was a silhouette against the hall-light.

PHILIP: This is preposterous! I tell you it wasn't me.

DUNNE: Can you suggest who else it could have been? Some visitor, perhaps?

PHILIP: We *(indicating Trisha)* should have known about it, shouldn't we? Really, Inspector, I must protest... wasting all our time with the working of an old woman's over-fertile imagination!

DUNNE: *(firmly)* This is a murder enquiry, sir. As a prospective member of Her Majesty's Government I should have expected that you would be only too willing to assist the police with their enquiries.

PHILIP: Well, of course I am. Did she hear what the supposed conversation was about?

ROSE: She admits to being slightly deaf. All she knows is that the voices were raised - as if in argument.

PHILIP: And she said this took place fairly recently?

DUNNE: That is correct... and as there have been no other sightings...

CLIVE: Or *claimed* sightings.

DUNNE: ...I think we can assume that what we are talking about is a date near to the time of the murder - if not the actual date itself.

PHILIP: Which you said was?

DUNNE: On or about the twenty-fifth of September.

PHILIP: *(confidently)* That settles it... I wasn't here!

DUNNE: May I ask where you were, sir?

PHILIP: I was out of the country for a couple of weeks... on the Continent in connection with the family business. Tying up a few loose ends with regard to our European markets. All being well I shall be too busy in Westminster to devote much time to it in future.

DUNNE: Travelling around, were you, sir?

PHILIP: Most of the time - but mainly based in Paris.

CLIVE: *(lightly)* Some people have all the luck, don't they, Trish? Philip gallivanting around Paris and points East... Kay filming in the South of

13

France... whilst you and I...

DUNNE: *(interrupting; to Philip)* And of course this can all be confirmed... someone who can verify...?

PHILIP: *(interrupting; strongly)* Damn it, Chief Inspector, my word should be good enough. What do you think I am - some sort of criminal? Of course it can be confirmed... flight bookings... hotel reservations... car hire...

DUNNE: *(coolly)* Thank you, sir. Then it would seem Miss Braithwaite was mistaken - unless....

KAY: Unless what?

DUNNE: Unless the man in the photograph was here but the man he was talking to wasn't Mr Stanton. *(TRISHA reacts almost imperceptibly.)*

PHILIP: *(to her)* Was there another man here while I was away?

TRISHA: Of course... *(becoming the focus of attention)* the milkman, the postman - the butcher's boy...

DUNNE: *(with severity)* Mrs Stanton, this is a serious matter. Was there another man here late one evening?

PHILIP: *(as she hesitates)* Don't answer that! really, Inspector, you go too far. What you're suggesting...

DUNNE: I wasn't suggesting anything untoward and if you or your wife think otherwise then I apologize unreservedly. May I take it that there wasn't?

TRISHA: *(without hesitation)* Of course there wasn't.

PHILIP: *(to Dunne)* Now are you satisfied?

DUNNE: Perfectly, sir. *(to Trisha)* Thank you, madame. That will be all. I regret having delayed you and *(with a nod towards Kay and Clive)* your guests. Enjoy your meal.

PHILIP: I'll show you out. *(Moving to open the door R)*

DUNNE: Thank you.... and may the best man win.

PHILIP: *(checking)* Pardon?

DUNNE: The Bye-Election, sir. *(moving to door)* And don't you forget to register your vote, Sergeant - not after all that trouble Mrs Pankhurst went to. *(with a polite nod)* Good evening, all. *(He EXITS followed by ROSE and then*

PHILIP, who closes the door after him.)

CLIVE: *(with a sigh of relief)* At last! I thought he was never going to go. I could do with another drink after that. May I, Trish? *(Moving to the drinks table L with his empty glass.)*

TRISHA: Of course.

CLIVE: How about you? Kay?

KAY: *(as TRISHA shakes her head)* No, thanks. I found it quite exciting... "An Inspector Calls"! *(Rising and handing her empty glass to him.)*

CLIVE: *(pouring himself a drink)* The man's a fool... him and his dear old mum.

TRISHA: *(tensely)* Or else very clever.

KAY: *(lightly)* Now you can tell us - while Philip is out of the room... who was your mysterious lover? The one the lady with the dog saw talking to Alexander.

CLIVE: *(sharply as TRISHA hesitates nervously)* That wasn't funny, Kay! Take no notice of her, Trish. She acts like this whenever she's kept waiting... for food or anything else! *(he drinks)*

(SOUND OF DOOR CLOSING OFF R. There is a brief moment of tension before PHILIP ENTERS R.)

(finishing his drink) Let's be off, shall we? Before Kay starts throwing things! *(starting to move R)*

PHILIP: *(seriously)* Hang on a minute. *(closing door)* There's something I'd like to get cleared up.

KAY: Not more questions? *(sitting again on the settee L)*

PHILIP: *(confronting Trisha)* You're hiding something, aren't you?

TRISHA: *(unconvincingly)* I don't know what you mean, Philip.

PHILIP: I think you do. You've been acting rather oddly ever since I got back from Paris. He was here, wasn't he?

TRISHA: Who?

PHILIP: That man... the man in the photograph.

CLIVE: Come off it, Philip! You're not taking what that Inspector said seriously, are you? He's a joke - and to think that's what we pay taxes for! Mind you, they can handcuff me to that Sergeant and throw away the key any time.

KAY: *(ironically)* And then what!?

PHILIP: *(to Trisha)* You recognised him from the photograph, didn't you? That business about the face of evil!

TRISHA: So he has... I mean - the photograph. Kay thought so... *(to her)* didn't you?

PHILIP: *(before she can speak)* You're lying, Trisha. I can always tell... you're not very good at it. *(after a brief pause)* Well?

CLIVE: *(as TRISHA rises uneasily)* Come of it, Philip! You're surely going to accept Trisha's word against that of some old woman with a dog? Leave it, for Heaven's sake, and let's go and eat. My stomach thinks my throat's been cut.

PHILIP: Just a minute. *(to Trisha)* You still haven't answered me. *(forcefully)* Was that man here or not?

TRISHA: *(losing self-control)* Yes, he was here! Now are you satisfied?

PHILIP: Not by a long chalk! Why didn't you tell me? Who was he? What did he want?

CLIVE: It sounds like "Twenty Questions"!

KAY: Shut up, Clive! This is getting interesting. *(to Trisha)* What did he want?

TRISHA: To see Philip.

PHILIP: *(as KAY looks questioningly at him)* I wasn't here.

TRISHA: That's what I told him.

PHILIP: And then?

TRISHA: He went away.

PHILIP: Just like that!? What about the argument?

TRISHA: There was no argument.

KAY: But the Inspector said that woman...

PHILIP: Miss Braithwaite.

KAY: ...told his Sergeant that voices were raised as if arguing.

TRISHA: And also that she was rather deaf.

PHILIP: What about the other man?

TRISHA: *(stealing a half-glance towards Clive)* There was no other man. She was mistaken. After all, it was dark.

PHILIP: And are you telling me that's all there was to it? Did he give his name? *(she shakes her head)* Or why he wanted to see me?

TRISHA: *(again shaking her head)* His English wasn't very good. It sounded to me as if he might be German.

PHILIP: *(glancing towards Clive)* German!?

KAY: *(noticing the glance)* Do you think he might be someone you and Clive knew - in Germany?

CLIVE: *(sarcastically)* There are only some nineteen million or so of them... admittedly not all male. Well, if that's it...

PHILIP: *(to Trisha)* So why didn't you tell me when I got back?

TRISHA: *(weakly)* I forgot. It didn't seem important.

PHILIP: Well, it's damned-well important now! The man's been murdered! And you lied to the police. Why?

CLIVE: I should have thought that was obvious.

PHILIP: *(sarcastically)* Even to me, you mean? Why don't you enlighten me, Holmes?

CLIVE: *(ignoring his sarcasm)* What good would it have done? No name... or why he came?

PHILIP: It would have helped the police... confirmed that he had been in the vicinity.

CLIVE: *(pertinently)* And looking for you! More questions involving you in a murder enquiry.

PHILIP: But I'm not involved!

KAY: Clive's right - though I hate to admit it.! The Press would have a field-day if they got wind of it, especially the less-responsible tabloids. Surely that's the last thing you'd want just now - with the Bye-Election coming up?

PHILIP: *(thoughtfully)* Yes, you're both right - in that respect. *(to Trisha)* Was that why you said you hadn't seen him?

TRISHA: Of course, darling. Why else?

PHILIP: I suppose I should thank you... although I really can't condone you not telling the police the truth. Apart from the strictly moral aspect it could be dangerous. If they come across someone lending credence to that old woman's story they'll be back - you can rest assured on that - and next time they won't be so easily put off.

CLIVE: *(easily)* Well, let's worry about that if and when it happens.

PHILIP: I shall be the one doing the worrying. You're in the clear, aren't you? *(jokingly)* You have got an alibi, I suppose? Was Kay at home?

KAY: About a month ago? No, I was filming on location in the South of France, as Clive said.. Very nice too! *(to Clive)* I got the most marvellous all-over tan, didn't I? Well, almost all over!

> *** Jack, Is this not a re-statement of the same information (South of France) given on page 13? Ian****

PHILIP: *(to Clive)* So you were on your own... or is that an indiscreet question?

CLIVE: Most indiscreet. But unfortunately my only companion was my word-processor - which I've programmed not to talk.

TRISHA: How's the latest book going?

KAY: Let's say that I still have to keep working if we're still to keep eating.

CLIVE: *(lightly)* Pay no attention - I'm halfway through the final draft. And speaking of eating...

PHILIP: Yes, you're right, we really must go. Another drink anyone?

KAY: *(as TRISHA and CLIVE indicate refusal)* I shouldn't mind one for the road. But I hate drinking alone.

PHILIP: *(moving to drinks table L)* In that case...

CLIVE: *(to Trisha)* Looks as if we both married alcoholics!

PHILIP: *(starting to pour drinks)* I can't get over the coincidence.

KAY: That we're both alcoholics?

PHILIP: That the man came here asking for me and a month or so later his body is found not far away. *(TRISHA moves to sit in the easy-chair RC as he hands a drink to Kay.)*

KAY: Thanks. Yes, it's a good job you weren't here, Philip, or else you'd probably be Suspect Number One.

CLIVE: Coincidences do happen all the time. As a matter of fact my new book's built around one. That's all it could be, isn't it? I mean, you weren't here and the police are never going to think that Trish could have done it... smashed in the back of his skull... dragged the body and dumped it in the car boot. Not a big man like that... then drive off...

PHILIP: *(about to drink)* What did you say?

CLIVE: I said the police would never believe...

PHILIP: *(putting glass down)* How do you know he was a big man?

CLIVE: What?

PHILIP: How do you know how big he was?

CLIVE: The police said...

PHILIP: No, they didn't. I'm certain they never mentioned his height or how much they estimated that he weighed.

CLIVE: *(starting to bluster)* I was judging from the photograph.

PHILIP: The head only... which you scarcely glanced at.

CLIVE: It must have been an assumption.

PHILIP: What size would you say he was, Trisha?

CLIVE: *(as she hesitates)* Can't you leave it...? Just leave it alone!

KAY: *(puzzled)* What are you getting so worked up about?

CLIVE: *(losing control)* I am not worked up! I only want to forget about the whole thing! That's all.

KAY: *(accusingly)* You were here, weren't you?

CLIVE: Are you mad!? Of course I wasn't here. Why should I have been here?

KAY: That's exactly what I'm wondering.

PHILIP: *(quietly)* Were you here, Clive?

CLIVE: I said "No", didn't I?

PHILIP: I don't think I believe you.

KAY: Neither do I.

PHILIP: Was Clive here, Trisha?

CLIVE: *(wildly)* Oh, all right! Yes, I was here. Are you satisfied?

PHILIP: No. Why were you here?

CLIVE: It was an impulse. I couldn't make any headway with the book - writer's block, I suppose. Kay was in France. I felt that I had to get away... that a change of air might do the trick. So I decided to drive up... see my old Army mate... reminisce about old times.

PHILIP: Sounds as if it could have been a good idea. Too bad you didn't 'phone in advance... could have saved you a long wasted journey.

CLIVE: Like I said, it was an impulse. But you're right - I should have 'phoned.

KAY: *(to Clive)* You didn't tell me you'd been up here.

CLIVE: No, I didn't, did I?

KAY: Why not?

CLIVE: *(too glibly)* Guess it must have slipped my memory... *(smiling)* was my journey really necessary?

KAY: You tell me - was it?

CLIVE: Oh, all right... I didn't want you carrying on.

KAY: About what?

CLIVE: About not pressing on with the book... running away from it... not sticking to my task!

PHILIP: *(to him)* But you didn't just turn around and drive back down South again, did you?

CLIVE: Not straight away, no. It was quite late in the day when I got here. Trish insisted that I should stay the night. I said I'd go to a hotel but she...

PHILIP: Insisted?

CLIVE: That's right.

PHILIP: So you drove back the next day?

CLIVE: *(glancing at Trisha)* Not the next day, no.

TRISHA: He stayed two nights. I asked Clive to... it was company for me - and with Kay being away.

KAY: *(derisively)* It was all very convenient!

CLIVE: *(defensively)* It was a good job I was here... when that man turned up - asking for Philip. Anything might have happened to Trisha.

PHILIP: What did happen? Presumably it was you Miss Braithwaite saw talking to him? What were you arguing about?

CLIVE: We weren't exactly arguing. I was trying to convince him that I wasn't you.

KAY: Although it must have looked that way!

PHILIP: So he wasn't someone who knew me?

CLIVE: Not personally, no. I suppose he might have got that impression... Trish and I being alone in the house together.

PHILIP: *(to Trisha)* I'm beginning to see why you didn't tell me... *(coldly)* not important, was it? *(to Clive)* I'm sorry, Clive, but I don't believe you'd drive all the way up here, ostensibly to see me... to reminisce about old times... without first ensuring that I'd be here. An impulse, you say? I know you too well - it's totally out of character. You're far too cold-blooded... impulsive you are not.

CLIVE: You think so?

PHILIP: I know so!

CLIVE: *(with a weak grin towards Trisha)* Then we might as well come clean. Trish 'phoned me.

PHILIP: *(looking at her)* What!?

CLIVE: Told me you were away and asked about Kay. When I told her that she was away Trish suggested that I should come up for a couple of days.

KAY: I thought it was nights!

PHILIP: *(astounded)* Are you telling me that you... and Trisha...?

KAY: *(surprised)* Philip! Don't say you never knew... never even guessed?

PHILIP: *(stunned)* No, never. Since when?

KAY: Since you were both stationed in Germany, wasn't it, Clive? Along with your respective wives. I always suspected there was something going on between them.

TRISHA: *(to Philip)* There was nothing to it, really. And it was a long time ago.

PHILIP: But you suddenly decided to rekindle the glowing embers? *(furiously; to Clive)* I ought to thrash you out of this house!

CLIVE: Oh, for God's sake, don't be so bloody melodramatic! You should be thanking me.

PHILIP: *(with incredulity)* Thanking you!? For sleeping with my wife? That *was* the object of the exercise, wasn't it?

CLIVE: For saving your life.

PHILIP: Oh, do me a favour!

CLIVE: I did. The man came here armed with a gun - to kill you!

PHILIP: Do you expect me to fall for that? I don't know him... never seen him in my whole life!

CLIVE: It's true. tell him, Trisha, tell him it's true!

TRISHA: *(quietly)* I saw the gun, Philip.

KAY: But why? *(to Philip)* Why should he want to kill you?

PHILIP: It's your husband's over-fertile imagination inventing a story to cover his sordid little affair with my wife.

CLIVE: They found the body, didn't they? Did I invent that?

PHILIP: No, but you're taking full advantage of it, aren't you? And dead men tell no tales!

CLIVE: That's right, they don't. Another good reason why you should thank me.

PHILIP: Is that supposed to mean something to me? *(after a brief pause)* Let's get this straight... are you trying to tell me that you killed him?

CLIVE: I'm not trying, Philip - I *did* kill him.

KAY: Clive! You're joking, aren't you?

PHILIP: *(to Trisha)* Is this true? *(she nods silently)* I can't believe I'm hearing this! Why? Why on earth should you kill him? If it was me he was after?

CLIVE: To keep him quiet for one thing.

PHILIP: And the other?

CLIVE: He was threatening to kill Trisha... that was after I'd finally convinced him that I wasn't you.

PHILIP: *(sitting; stunned)* It's like a nightmare! It makes no sense... a complete stranger comes intending to kill me - or so you say - and then threatens to kill Trisha. Why? *(to Trisha when CLIVE remains silent)* Do you know why?

TRISHA: Not really, no. When the man started to get nasty Clive told me to lock myself in the bathroom. After that I didn't see what happened. Later on Clive said it was about something that happened in Germany - before Kay and I went out to join you both.

PHILIP: *(puzzled)* Something that... but I'm positive I've never seen the man - never! *(to Clive)* What was it?

CLIVE: *(quietly)* Leave it, Philip.

PHILIP: *(rising quickly)* How can I damned-well leave it!? You say you killed a man in this house... it *was* here, I suppose? Firstly you involved my wife and now you've got me involved with the police - probably as a suspect. That's all I need right now. I want to know why... I insist on knowing what it's all about!

CLIVE: *(reluctantly)* Very well - if you insist. Do you remember Helga?

PHILIP: *(trying to conceal a nervous reaction)* Helga?

CLIVE: Helga Schwartz.

TRISHA: Who's Helga?

CLIVE: She was a... she worked in a bar that Philip and I used to frequent when off duty in Berlin - before the unit moved out into those barracks where you and Kay joined us in the Married Quarters.

PHILIP: *(with mock indifference)* Oh, *that* Helga!

KAY: You've never mentioned her before - either of you.

CLIVE: *(with a shrug)* She was a refugee from East Berlin before the Wall came down. Lucky she wasn't killed.

KAY: Lucky for you!?

CLIVE: She only had eyes for Philip.

TRISHA: Did she?

PHILIP: *(curtly to Clive)* So where does that man come in?

CLIVE: He was her husband, Dieter Schwartz.

PHILIP: *(quickly)* She told me he was dead.

CLIVE: I think you'd find that what Helga actually said was that she presumed he was dead. he'd got into some trouble with the Soviets some time after the war - black marketeering, or drugs, something like that - and had got hauled off to a labour camp, probably in Siberia. She'd never heard from him again.

KAY: But he wasn't dead?

CLIVE: Not then he wasn't.

PHILIP: But he is now! So why did he come?

CLIVE: Look, are you sure you want Trish to hear this?

PHILIP: She was here, wasn't she? What doesn't she know?

CLIVE: What I didn't tell her. How's that for friendship?

PHILIP: I'm touched! What did this Dieter Schwartz want?

CLIVE: In your absence - an eye for an eye.

PHILIP: What the devil does that mean?

CLIVE: A wife for a wife!

PHILIP: I didn't kill Helga.

CLIVE: No - he did!

(There is a general reaction.)

PHILIP: What!?

TRISHA: I said he was evil.

KAY: Killed his own wife!? Why?

PHILIP: *(recovering slightly)* Yes, why?

CLIVE: It appears that many years later he was released and set about trying to find Helga - and his son.

PHILIP: She didn't have a son!

CLIVE: Not when we pulled out of Berlin, no. Did she tell you she was pregnant?

PHILIP: No, she didn't. *(In response to TRISHA's questioning look)* I swear I didn't know! *(after a brief thoughtful pause; to Clive)* Are you trying to say...? It could have been anyone. It could have been you!

CLIVE: No such luck, old boy.

PHILIP: But you tried - she told me you tried.

CLIVE: *(to Kay)* Without success.

KAY: It's the thought that counts!

CLIVE: Not where pregnancy is concerned. Schwartz said she told him that you were the father - when he finally tracked her down. Apparently she tried to tell him she'd been raped.

TRISHA: Philip!

PHILIP: *(hotly)* It's a downright lie!

CLIVE: I believe you. Whether or not he believed her, I don't know. I suspect it would have made no difference either way. Not hard to understand the toll that all those years had exacted on him and then to find... he must have been unhinged, not really knowing what he was doing. He shot her, he said... and then the boy.

(Again there is general reaction.)

Then he set out with only one thing on his mind... revenge!

KAY: But how did he know...?

CLIVE: Helga must have given him Philip's name. Probably beat it out of her.

PHILIP: *(with feeling)* Oh, God! *(to Trisha)* I'm not proud of what I did but I'm not ashamed either. I really did care for her and felt sure that she did too.

TRISHA: Not ashamed? What a hypocrite you are!

CLIVE: Heaven above knows how he managed to find you - or rather *didn't* find you... still, it hardly matters now, does it?

PHILIP: That bastard! If I had been here I might have been tempted to kill him myself. How did you...?

CLIVE: Perhaps it would be as well for you not to know too much.

PHILIP: Yes, you're probably right. Wouldn't want to end up as an accessory after the fact. That would be the end of my parliamentary career before it had even begun!

CLIVE: Lucky for you I was here, wasn't it? In a manner of speaking.

PHILIP: *(with a look towards Trisha)* In a manner of speaking, yes.

KAY: So what happens now?

CLIVE: Now I suggest that we finally eat.

KAY: I'm not hungry any more - certainly not to eat in your company. First you admit to screwing Trisha behind my back, then you calmly announce that you've killed a man - having previously lied to the police so that suspicion fell on Philip.

CLIVE: *(nastily)* What did you expect me to do... say "it's a fair cop, I did it"? Anyway, whose side are you on?

KAY: Not yours, that's for sure!

CLIVE: It's all your precious Philip's fault. If he'd kept his fly done up none of this would have happened.

KAY: There's no need to be uncouth.

CLIVE: *(sarcastically)* Sorry, I'm sure!

PHILIP: I still don't understand why you had to kill him.

CLIVE: I told you - he was threatening to kill Trisha.

PHILIP: I only have your word for that.

CLIVE: And Trisha's.

PHILIP: Who was locked upstairs in the bathroom. You also said it was to keep him quiet. Quiet about what?

CLIVE: What do you think? Did you want it splashing on the front pages, and on the telly - about you and Helga and the kid?

PHILIP: So you did it all for me?

CLIVE: And Trisha.

PHILIP: And Trisha. Tell me, Clive - that last night we were in Berlin, do you remember? I had to take over as Duty Officer unexpectedly when Teddy Crowther was whipped off to hospital with what was euphemistically described as a self-inflicted wound... with ladies present I'll leave it at that.

CLIVE: *(cautiously)* Yes...?

PHILIP: I had a small present for Helga. Nothing much - a couple of pairs of stockings. I asked you to give them to her.

CLIVE: Oh, yes, now I remember. She was very grateful.

PHILIP: Was she!? How grateful, Clive? Grateful enough to invite you into bed?

CLIVE: *(uneasily)* I've already said - she only had eyes for you.

PHILIP: *(forcefully)* Which you could never stomach, could you? Forbidden fruit... always that bit sweeter, isn't it? Oh, sure, you gave her the stockings in the bar, but then, when she'd finished working, you walked her back to that squalid little one-roomed flat she called home, didn't you? *(no response)* Didn't you!?

CLIVE: Yes, I may have done.

PHILIP: Then you raped her, didn't you? There's no way she would have let you otherwise.

TRISHA: *(to Clive)* Is it true?

PHILIP: Of course it's true. Look at him! Why else would he have killed Schwartz? Because he was afraid that he had been the father of Helga's child!

KAY: *(scathingly)* You're pathetic!

(DOORBELL RINGS off R. ALL "freeze".)

PHILIP: *(moving to the window and holding the curtain aside to look off R)* The police are back.

TRISHA: *(nervously)* What are you going to do?

PHILIP: Let them in, of course. *(moving towards door R)*

CLIVE: *(confidently)* Probably come to take you in for questioning.

KAY: Why should they? Philip has an alibi. We spent a few days together in Paris after I'd finished filming.

CLIVE: *(reacting together with TRISHA)* He still could have been that kid's father! *(Doorbell rings again off R.)*

PHILIP: *(opening door; with a smile)* Haven't you wondered why we've never had children? Ask Trisha! *(EXITS R)*

KAY: *(unable to resist a wry laugh)* Oh, Clive, if you could only see your face!

CURTAIN